Cultivators
Go to Work

Jennifer Boothroyd

Lerner Publications ◆ Minneapolis

To Brent Hennen and his farming family

New Holland is a registered trademark of CNH International and is used under license.

Lerner Publications Company
A division of Lerner Publishing Group, Inc.
241 First Avenue North
Minneapolis, MN 55401 USA

For reading levels and more information, look up this title at www.lernerbooks.com.

Main body text set in Billy Infant Semibold 17/23.
Typeface provided by SparkyType.

Library of Congress Cataloging-in-Publication Data

Names: Boothroyd, Jennifer, 1972- author.
Title: Cultivators go to work / Jennifer Boothroyd.
Description: Minneapolis : Lerner Publications, 2018. | Series: Farm machines at work | Includes
    bibliographical references and index.
Identifiers: LCCN 2017047852 (print) | LCCN 2017051408 (ebook) | ISBN 9781541526068 (eb pdf) |
    ISBN 9781541525993 (lb : alk. paper) | ISBN 9781541527676 (pb : alk. paper)
Subjects: LCSH: Cultivators—Juvenile literature.
Classification: LCC S683 (ebook) | LCC S683 .B66 2018 (print) | DDC 631.5/1—dc23

LC record available at https://lccn.loc.gov/2017047852

Manufactured in the United States of America
1-44567-35498-1/22/2018

TABLE OF CONTENTS

1
FARMS NEED
CULTIVATORS

Heavy cultivators such as this one dig deep into the ground, while lighter cultivators stir up the top of the soil.

Farmers use machines to make their work easier. Cultivators help with many different jobs on a farm. Farmers use cultivators to break up clumps of soil. Loose soil lets more water reach plant roots.

Cultivators also kill weeds near crops.
Some cultivators cut down weeds.
Others push weeds under the ground.

Cultivators are important farm machines.
They help farmers work larger fields.
Farmers can grow more crops such as corn,
wheat, and soybeans.

Weeds can take away nutrients and
water that crops need to grow.

EXPLORE THE
CULTIVATOR

A cultivator's frame hooks to a tractor. The tractor's large engine and wheels pull the cultivator through the field.

The frame holds the shanks. Shanks are sharp pieces of metal. They cut weeds and move the dirt.

Shanks can be long, pointy pieces or round discs.

Discs don't dig deep into the soil.

Some discs have spiky edges.
They help break up the soil.
The discs turn when they are
dragged across the ground.

A farmer pulls the cultivator carefully through the crop rows. Weeds get left behind or buried as the dirt is turned.

Springs on the cultivator move the shanks out of the way if they hit a rock.

3 CULTIVATORS ON THE FARM

Farmers use cultivators early in the growing season.

Loosened soil helps seeds grow better and faster.

Cultivators work with other farm machines. Farmers attach drip lines to cultivators. Nutrients or fertilizers flow through tubes and drip onto the soil.

Some planting machines have cultivator parts in them. The soil gets broken up and seeds are planted in one trip down the field. Making fewer trips saves time. It stops the soil from getting packed down.

This planting machine is called an air seeder.

Cultivators fold up in much the same way as this air seeder does.

Sometimes farmers need to take their cultivators on a road. Very wide cultivators fold up. This makes them safer on busy roads. It is also easier to fit the folded cultivators into a shed.

Long ago, farmers used hand tools to break up the ground. They worked one row at a time. It was hard work.

Later, people used horses to help with farmwork. The horses dragged simple cultivators through a field. Farmers could work more than one row at a time. Once tractors were invented, cultivators moved even faster.

Modern cultivators come in many sizes to fit the needs of different types of farms.

Most modern crop farms use cultivators. Some types of cultivators protect the soil from erosion, or the washing away of soil. Erosion is bad for crops.

In the future, cultivator robots may work fields. The robots could move by themselves without a tractor. The farmer could control the robots with a computer.

Someday this cultivator may drive itself!

CULTIVATOR PARTS

hitch

frame

tire

shank

FUN CULTIVATOR FACTS

- Some cultivators weigh 2 tons (1,814 kg) or more. That's the same as an adult hippopotamus!

- One of the largest cultivators is 80 feet (24 m) wide. It cultivates more than forty rows at a time.

- People can use smaller cultivators in their yards and gardens. These cultivators may have only two to six shanks.

GLOSSARY

crop: a plant grown to eat

erosion: wearing away by wind or water

fertilizer: a substance added to soil to help plants grow

growing season: the time of year when plants grow well

nutrient: a substance that plants need to grow

shank: a piece of metal in a cultivator that gets dragged through the soil. Shanks can be long, pointy pieces or round discs.

soil: the top layer of dirt where plants grow

weed: an unwanted plant

FURTHER READING

Boothroyd, Jennifer. *Tractors Go to Work.* Minneapolis: Lerner Publications, 2019.

Dittmer, Lori. *Cultivators.* Mankato, MN: Creative Education, 2018.

Dufek, Holly. *Planters & Cultivators with Casey & Friends.* Austin, TX: Octane, 2016.

Growing Plants
http://www.pbs.org/parents/sid/activities/growing-plants/

Know Your Roots!
https://www.ars.usda.gov/oc/kids/whatinworld/roots/3drootshome/

Maimone, S. M. *Cultivators.* New York: Gareth Stevens, 2016.

EXPLORE MORE

Learn even more about cultivators! Scan the QR code to see photos and videos of cultivators in action.

READ ALL THE BOOKS IN THE
FARM MACHINES AT WORK SERIES!

Balers Go to Work

Cultivators Go to Work

Harvesters Go to Work

Skid Steers Go to Work

Sprayers Go to Work

Tractors Go to Work

INDEX

PHOTO ACKNOWLEDGMENTS

All images in this book are used with the permission of New Holland except:

Somchai Sanvongchaiya/Shutterstock.com, p. 9; Laszlo66/Shutterstock.com, p. 10; © USDA Photo by Lance Cheung, p. 12 (inset); Charles Brutlag/Shutterstock.com, p. 13; Sunny Forest/Shutterstock.com, p. 16 (corn field); USDA Photo, p. 16 (field workers); National Archives, p. 17; panic_attack/Getty Images, p. 18. Design elements: CHEMADAN/Shutterstock.com; LongQuattro/Shutterstock.com; pingebat/Shutterstock.com; enjoynz/DigitalVision Vectors/Getty Images.

Cover: New Holland